TOPI.

Twigs Way

SHIRE PUBLICATIONS

First published in Great Britain in 2010 by Shire Publications Ltd, Midland House, West Way, Botley, Oxford OX2 0PH, United Kingdom.
44-02 23rd Street, Suite 219, Long Island City, NY 11101 USA.

E-mail: shire@shirebooks.co.uk   www.shirebooks.co.uk

A CIP catalogue record for this book is available from the British Library.

Shire Library no. 580   •   ISBN-13: 978 0 74780 761 2

Twigs Way has asserted her right under the Copyright, Designs and Patents Act, 1988, to be identified as the author of this book.

Designed by Myriam Bell Design, France and typeset in Perpetua and Gill Sans.
Printed in China through Worldprint Ltd.

10 11 12 13 14   10 9 8 7 6 5 4 3 2 1

COVER IMAGE
A combination of crisp lines and visible branches gives the impression that this garden has been frozen in time.

TITLE PAGE IMAGE
Versailles topiary, oddly reminiscent of a poodle.

CONTENTS PAGE IMAGE
Topiary rabbits on the lawn. They are perhaps more welcome than the real thing!

ACKNOWLEDGEMENTS
The author would like to thank Philip Norman of The Garden Museum (London) for encouraging her to write this book and for providing many of the images. Also C. Stephen Briggs for providing the images of Klinkert nurseries and fascinating material on Welsh topiary, John Williams for the reference to Penpont lions, and Amoret Tanner for access to her collections.

Other illustrations are acknowledged as follows:

courtesy of Ashridge and Nick Thompson, page 18; Lucy Atkinson, page 4; Thomas Becker, page 7 (top); Stephen Briggs, pages 42 (top and right), and 43 (top); Michael Caffrey, cover; Cambridge University Library, pages 16 (all), 21, and 37 (bottom); Francesco Celano, page 14; Charles Drakew, page 8; Ewa Farrelly, page 7 (bottom); *Gardener's Chronicle*, page 40; Gardens of Easton Lodge, page 47; The Garden Museum, pages 26 (middle), 35, 41 (top), 43 (middle), 44–6 (all), 48, 52 (bottom), 59 (left), and 60 (top); Chris Goddard, page 30; Amanda Goode, page 6 (bottom); Ian Griffiths, page 36 (top); Rory O'Brien, page 3; Enrico Sapignoli, page 17; Ben Sutherland, page 29; Amoret Tanner, pages 6 (top), 26 (top), 43 (bottom), 50–1 (all), 56, 59 (right), and 60 (bottom); Victoria and Albert Museum, page 27.

All other images are from the author's collection.

GLOSSARY

Parterre	An elaborately decorated area of flat ground using low clipped plants, grass and gravels or coloured earths.
Allée	A formal walk between two avenues of trees or high hedges, which was an essential part of French baroque gardens.
Arbutus unedo	Strawberry tree
Prunus laurocerasus	Cherry laurel

CONTENTS

INTRODUCTION

Topiary has always been a divisive garden art. Some have praised it as the highest achievement of the gardener's skill, whilst others have declared that it is merely a defacement and distortion of nature. Nicholson's *Dictionary of Gardening* (1887) described it as an 'absurd fashion of cutting and torturing trees into all sorts of fantastic shapes'. The current *Oxford English Dictionary* is more restrained, defining it as 'the art or practice of clipping shrubs or trees into ornamental shapes'. Whether high skill or absurd fashion, topiary, or 'vegetable sculpture', has a long history. The word itself is derived from the Ancient Greek *topos* (τόπος) or 'place', which forms the root of words such as 'topography'. The Romans used the same root to form 'topiarus', meaning an ornamental landscape designer. Thought to have originated with the Romans, clipping shrubs into shapes has always been an important element in formal gardens. In Tudor and Elizabethan gardens the clipped knot was essential to the garden, as well as cones or 'pyramidal' shapes and figures. The popularity of topiary and all things clipped waned with the coming of the 'English Landscape' movement in the mid-eighteenth century and the liberating force of Dame Nature. Dragons of ivy and 'old maids in wormwood' (see page 30) were lampooned and even the relatively inoffensive boxwood balls and cones of the 'Dutch' style garden were banished by the mid-eighteenth century.

As the years moved on, so fashions turned, and the late nineteenth and early twentieth centuries saw topiary literally reach new heights. Plump green peacocks, smug cats, cake-stands and chessmen added an 'old-fashioned' air to the flowing herbaceous borders and neatly mown lawns of countless country houses. Supposedly traditional designs were created anew and many an 'old Dutch' garden freshly planted. Clipping became a 'craft' and was taken up as such by the Arts and Crafts Movement. Carefully woven 'forms' pre-shaped into the most popular designs allowed even amateur practitioners to create complex pieces, and topiary became the delight of the cottage garden as much as the country house.

Modern topiary takes many forms and styles, from the figurative to the abstract, with flowing forms increasingly popular and Japanese cloud forms

Opposite:
Cottage garden topiary, usually of single pieces, remains popular. Here a peacock has become a proud chicken.

5

Almost anything is possible with topiary, even the Garden of Eden (complete with serpent)!

Less ambitious, but sitting pretty in its overflowing cottage garden, is this fledgling topiary bird.

being fashionable, despite substantial price tags for these venerable plants. Figure work has become even more quirky and wide-ranging, with crocodiles of box lurking in the undergrowth and dragons occupying the smallest of suburban gardens. A recent judge at the famous RHS Chelsea show

Left: Few gardens can accommodate an entire herd of elephants. These are at the King's Summer Palace in Thailand.

confidently announced a revival of the crisp green clipped forms in 'credit-crunched' gardens, turning on its head the usual adage that topiary is costly and labour intensive.

In 1904 W. Gibson (writing in Charles Curtis's *The Book of Topiary*) declared that 'In writing on the Topiary garden, I have perhaps made it appear to some of those who may read it as hideously unnatural, and I am aware that there are plenty who maintain that this is a style of gardening that has little to recommend or encourage about it.' Little was he to know of the revival that would follow, or the continued popularity of topiary some 100 years later! Whether art, craft or horticultural whimsy, topiary is here to stay.

Right:
This bizarre topiary garden uses a combination of figures, animals and free flow to create a wonderful mix of shapes.

CLASSICAL TOPIARY

D ESPITE the Greek origins of its name, European topiary appears to have commenced with the Romans. For the Romans '*opus topiarus*' or 'work of topiary' was a much broader term, meaning the art of creating the garden or landscape as a whole. Pliny the Elder in his *Naturalis Historia* (*c.* AD 77–9) states specifically that '*nemora tonsilia*' (variously translated as 'barbered groves' or clipped arbours, which we would now refer to as topiary) had been introduced about 80 years before his writing. This invention of clipped work he attributes to Caius Matius Calvena, 'a friend of his late majesty Augustus'. Pliny himself does not seem to have cared much for this clipped work or for dwarfing and stunting generally, calling the dwarf plane produced by 'a method of planting and lopping' an unhappy abortion. Many of the *topiarii*, or gardeners and garden designers to the Roman aristocratic classes, were in fact Greek, and it is possible that Caius Matius was merely taking credit for the work of his Greek gardener!

Despite Pliny's distaste for the unnatural, the fashion for '*nemora tonsilia*' and other clipped work appears to have caught on quite quickly. In the first century AD, Pliny the Younger wrote to his friend Domitius Apollinaris describing his country villa in Tuscany. In the letter he goes into considerable detail about his gardens, and mentions not only clipped box edging but also topiary figures. The vision he gives of Roman frivolity, with animals parading in evergreen form and the gardener busy clipping his own name in box letters, has intrigued garden historians for many years. Pliny does not actually use the word 'topiary', referring instead to 'box cut into many shapes' (*concisus in plurimas species distinctusque buxo*):

In front of the portico is a sort of terrace, edged with box and shrubs cut into different shapes. You descend, from the terrace, by an easy slope adorned with the figures of animals

The double line of box hedging at Fishbourne Roman Palace, recreated on the basis of archaeological excavation.

in box, facing each other, to a lawn … this is surrounded by a walk enclosed with evergreens, shaped into a variety of forms. Beyond it is the gestatio, laid out in the form of a circus running round the multiform box-hedge and the dwarf-trees, which are cut quite close… In one place you have a little meadow, in another the box is cut in a thousand different forms, sometimes into letters, expressing the master's name, sometimes the artificer's, whilst here and there rise little obelisks with fruit-trees alternatively intermixed, and then on a sudden, in the midst of this elegant regularity, you are surprised with an imitation of the negligent beauties of rural nature.

Other recorded examples of Roman topiary work include a hunting scene with a pack of hounds chasing a fox, and another of a fleet of ships clipped in cypress. In the seventeenth century wooden trellis fences were created echoing these classical originals, also with ships in full sail.

Box clippings found during excavations at Roman sites in Britain such as Frocester (Glos), Silchester (Hants) and Winterton (Lincs) suggest that there may have been some form of topiary at these sites. Shears of the type still used for clipping box topiary have also been found at several Roman sites across Europe, although whether these were purely for topiary or had other purposes in the garden and house is not known. Unfortunately no images of Roman topiary survive, although the popular 'spiral' form in pots is often known as Roman-style.

At the famous site of Fishbourne (Sussex) archaeological evidence indicates that there was clipped hedging in a complex pattern. The actual planting trenches had been filled with dark organic earth, allowing archaeologists to distinguish them from the lighter coloured gravelly subsoils. The double hedge lines alternate between straight lines and semicircles, creating 'alcoves' for statues or seating. The hedge has been re-planted in box.

A giant 'B' at Levens Hall, (Westmorland), probably rather larger than Pliny had in mind!

KNOT TOPIARY: MEDIEVAL AND TUDOR ENGLAND

WITH THE WANING of the Roman Empire came a decline in clipped work, and representations of medieval topiary indicate that only simple forms were attempted. Paintings of the fifteenth century depict standards with long stems topped by simple balls, or the 'estrade'. The latter was a type of tiered cake-stand, but rather than being produced primarily by clipping branches, the pliable new growth was woven around wooden frames. A wide variety of woody plants was used for these, and scented herbs were popular choices, including santolina, lavender, teucrium (wall germander), rosemary, hyssop and bay. Paintings from the Netherlands and northern Europe show these simple forms grown in low pots and placed around the edges of walled gardens.

In England a fashion for knot gardens, mazes and labyrinths kept the art of clipping alive until the revival of figurative topiary in the sixteenth century and the eventual golden age of seventeenth-century topiary. Knot gardens, composed of low hedges planted to form complex patterns or entwined initials, are a form of topiary. These gardens were extremely popular in the sixteenth and early seventeenth century in all sizes of gardens. Pattern books contained suggestions for layouts, often taken directly from embroidery books or sometimes copied from architectural patterning on ceilings. Small gardens might contain just one 'knot', whilst larger areas typically had four- or eight-square knot gardens in pairs. The more complex the patterns, the more skillful was the gardener and the wealthier and more fashionable the garden owner. George Cavendish (1500–61) described the gardens of his master Cardinal Wolsey as: 'The knotts so enknotted, it cannot be exprest, With

'The True Lovers Knott' from Stephen Blake's *The Compleat Gardeners Practice* (1664).

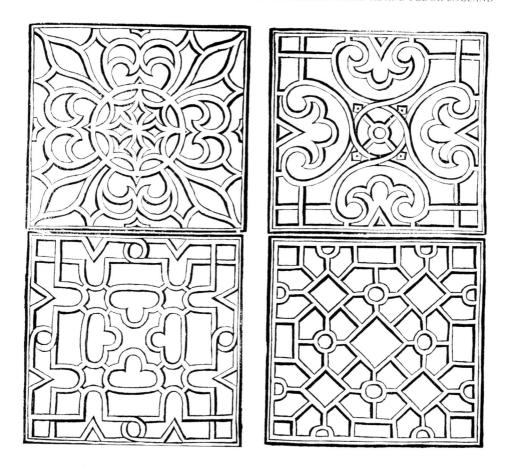

arbours and alyes so pleasant and so dulcet [sweet], the pestilent ayres with flavours to repulse'. The gardens of Cardinal Wolsey lay around his house at Hampton Court, where two hundred years later the topiary 'Dutch' gardens of William and Mary were to set a fashion that swept England. The duke of Buckingham in 1502 is recorded as having made special payments to his gardeners for 'diligence in making knots and for clipping of knots.'

Instructions on planting and designing knot gardens were available in contemporary gardening and estate management books such as Thomas Hill's *The Gardener's Labyrinth* (1577) and William Lawson's *A New Orchard and Garden* with *The Country Housewife's Garden* (1618). Hill's popular work included a section on 'Herbers, Knots and Mazes, cunningly handled for the beautifying of gardens', whilst Lawson also provided plans for knots. Lawson recommends using a mix of flowers and herbs within the knots, including roses, cowslips,

A variety of patterns for knot gardens taken from William Lawson's *The Country Housewife's Garden* (1618).

This early to mid-seventeenth century style knot garden and central topiary piece in holly has been planted at The Garden Museum, London. The garden commemorates the John Tradescants (father and son) gardeners and plantsmen and was designed by Lady Salisbury.

peonies, daisies, clove-gilliflowers, pinks, and lilies, whilst the actual knots themselves could add further colour and scent by being made of rosemary, lavender, hyssop, sage, or thyme. Some gardeners and housewives made up their own devices or patterns according to Lawson. If the housewife were lacking in imagination, she might also use Stephen Blake's book *The Compleat Gardeners Practice* (1664), where he includes the 'True Lovers Knott', although he sadly explains that 'to ty it in mariage was never my lott'. Most of the scented herbs used to create the knots and mazes would have died back in winter leaving a bare garden, and also needed to be re-planted every few years. It is not surprising therefore that by the mid-sixteenth century these scented herbs had been joined by more hardy evergreens.

This seventeenth-century style knot and topiary garden at Hatfield House was one of the first recreations of this type of garden and was carefully researched by Lady Salisbury.

Box, which was to become so popular in the late seventeenth century, was rarely used in the Tudor and Elizabethan knot garden. In his 1578 book *A Niew Herball*, Henry Lyte described box as being 'very hurtful for the brayne when it is but smelled', and twenty years later John Gerard called the smell 'evil and loathsome'. Queen Anne was later to make the same complaint when she inherited Hampton Court from her brother William, and legend has it that she insisted on the box being removed. In *Le Jardin de Plaisir* (translated into English in 1670) André Mollet commented that there are two sorts of box, great box (wood box) and dwarf box: 'I know that in this country [England] most part have an aversion to all kind of Box by reason of its strong scent and chiefly the biggest, but that happens only when it is

suffered to grow high, for being kept short and low, it scarce smells at all, especially the dwarf box'. Box is mentioned favourably by Gervase Markham in his *The English Husbandman* (1613) along with privet, but the book is an almost direct translation from a French work and cannot be relied on to indicate what was commonly used in England. French knot patterns and *parterres* were heavily influenced by what was happening in Renaissance Italy and southern Europe, where designs were complex and gardens more formal, necessitating plants that could be easily clipped to small precise shapes.

Box is often used in modern knot gardens as it needs less maintenance and gives an all-year pattern, but it was rarely used in the Tudor garden.

A modern knot and topiary garden uses dramatic colours to add to the varied textures and shapes.

13

TOPIARY RE-BORN: THE EUROPEAN RENAISSANCE

R ENAISSANCE ITALY led the revival of complex figurative topiary. Basing designs and ideas on Roman texts, owners of Renaissance villa gardens created animal and human figures and scenes as well as architectural forms such as small temples or urns. Although the inspiration for these was ultimately supposed to be taken from the classical, they were also inspired by one of the most mysterious texts popular in the fifteenth and sixteenth centuries, the wonderfully titled *Hypnerotomachia Poliphili* (*Poliphilo's Strife of Love in a Dream*). First printed in Venice in 1499, the story relates the tale of Poliphilo as he pursues his lover Polia through a dreamlike landscape of oceans, islands, pleasure grounds and gardens. As the story reaches its climax with their reconciliation at the Fountain of Venus, the lovers pass through an increasingly elaborate and rich series of gardens on the dream Island of Cythera. Representing the Renaissance ideal, the gardens include a wealth of topiary figures and forms, many outrageous in scale and complexity. *Hypnerotomachia Poliphili* first appeared in English in 1592 (and then only in part) but it was undoubtedly well known amongst the aristocracy before that. Even those who could not read the text could admire the illustrations of topiary at its most magnificent.

The topiary depicted in the illustrations is such that a modern topiarist would struggle to compete: a man standing astride, balancing castles in each hand, which in turn are topped by an arch and centre piece; a collonaded fountain topped with birds and canopy; a hedge of clipped cypress and pine; and wreaths and circles. In even more splendid gardens Poliphilo sees, we are told, 'plants of gold and glass in imitation of topiary', 'exceeding a man's imagination or belief', so that even the noble evergreen is dispensed with in favour of gems.

The visions of Poliphilo are thought to be based on real Italian gardens that the author had visited. But who was the author? The book has been variously attributed to an otherwise little-known Dominican priest, Brother Francesco Colonna, the more famous humanist architect Leon Battista Alberti, or even the fabulously wealthy Lorenzo de Medici. Lorenzo and

Opposite: The 'Giardino segreto' at the Villa Doria with its restored seventeenth-century clipped gardens.

Alberti lead us back to the actual villas and villa gardens of Italy. In 1452 Alberti wrote a book called *De re aedificatoria*, which he dedicated to Lorenzo de Medici. In it he describes a Renaissance countryside villa, using as his ideal a Roman garden complete with boxwood and topiaries. Lorenzo de Medici himself was a member of one of several influential families who owned such villa gardens in the countryside around Rome and Florence, and the dedication may indicate that he owned such a garden. In 1459, a few years after his book was printed, Alberti received orders to create a new villa and garden at Quaracchi for the Rucellai family, and other orders soon followed. In the fifteenth century the Villa Rucellai was described as containing clipped 'spheres, porticoes, temples, vases, urns, apes, donkeys, oxen, a bear, giants, men and women, warriors, a witch, philosophers, popes and cardinals'. The gardens of the Rucellai family set a trend and soon the gardens of the Villa

Above, above right, and below:
Just some of the fantastic topiary forms in the *Hypnerotomachia Poliphili*.

Lante in Viterbo, Castello Balduino at Montalto di Pavia, and the Villa Garzoni, near Collodi in Tuscany, were all replete with topiary forms and features. Some of these villa gardens still exist today and reflect the original influence of the Renaissance in their box *parterres*, clipped hedges, and topiary work, although none are as magnificent and complex as their historic descriptions suggest.

By the mid-seventeenth century, France led the way in formal garden design with vast and intricate 'embroidered *parterres*', avenues and *allées*, and of course topiary. As in the earlier Italian villas, clipped evergreens took two main forms: low intricate swirls of box hedging that formed part of the complex *parterre* patterns, and free-standing or potted topiary shapes.

The most famous garden designers of the period were the Frenchmen André le Nôtre, Claude Mollet and his son André Mollet. In André Mollet's book *Le Jardin de Plaisir* (1651) he describes the design of *allées*, palisades of clipped trees and topiary. Of embroidered knots or *parterres* he says, 'Those of box are more formed for the neat and small embroidery, because that the box can be planted and clipped into what shape one will'. Decorating the edges of these *parterres* will be 'marked places for cyprus trees, which must be kept always cropped neatly in a pyramidal form and not suffered to grow above five or seven foot at the most in height' and also 'flower Pots or small boxes of choice green trees, some clip't and crop't like Globes, others in Pyramidal form'.

André Mollet travelled widely, creating formal gardens in England in the 1620s and again in 1642 (for Queen Henrietta Maria at Wimbledon). In 1633 he designed a garden in Holland for Prince Frederick Henry of Orange at Huis Honselaarsdijk, where he created *parterres en broderie* that included the

The Villa Lante, Viterbo (Italy) still retains a crisply clipped formality in its Renaissance-inspired gardens.

lion rampant of the prince's coat-of-arms in turf and clipped box set in coloured gravels. In each garden, upright topiary of cones, balls, pillars and other forms complemented the low clipped box and what contemporaries described as 'topiary labyrinths'.

Clipped hedge mazes were also very popular in France in this period, with famous examples known at Versailles, Chantilly, Choisy-le-Roi, and Les Rochers. The maze at Versailles incorporated thirty-nine hydraulic figures illustrating Aesop's fables – but these were statues rather than greenery! André Mollet gave several examples of maze designs in his *Jardin de Plaisir*. John Evelyn, who visited Paris in 1643 (being of royalist sympathies, he spent much time abroad at this period), commented on the design and trimness of the box hedge at the Luxembourg Gardens and the 'labyrinth of cypresse' at Les Tuileries. Evelyn also visited Italy and saw the maze in the gardens of Count Vilmarini at Vicenza. This particular maze was described again in 1663 by another Englishman, Sir Phillip Skippon, who said it was planted with myrtle.

This 'lion rampant' at Ashridge, Herts, echoes the seventeenth-century clipped box at Huis Honselaarsdijk.

Louis XIV of France adored topiary and carried the art to extremes in the early eighteenth-century royal French gardens. His son, Louis XV, although less extrovert, continued the theme and even organised a famous 'Ball of the Clipped Yews', where courtiers came in yew head-dresses and masks. He met his future mistress Jeanne-Antoinette Poisson, later the Marquise de Pompadour, at this ball in 1745. Patterns for the popular topiary at Versailles were published in the eighteenth century and have been used in the recent restoration of the gardens.

Topiary work at Versailles.

THE GOLDEN AGE
OF ENGLISH TOPIARY:
1550–1700

ALTHOUGH 'clipped work' in the form of knots, mazes and labyrinths was popular in England in the first part of the sixteenth century, it is only from the 1550s onwards that we have any firm evidence for the use of topiary figures.

In his poem *The Historie of Graunde Amoure and la bell Pucle, called the Pastime of Plesure* (*c.* 1523) Stephen Hawes describes:

> … Flora painted and wrought curiously
> In divers knots of marvelous greatness
> Rampant lions stood by wonderfully
> Made all of herbs, with dulcet sweetness
> With many dragons of marvelous likeness.

Rampant or 'ramping' lions appear to have been a favourite of the topiarist. They are also mentioned in the nineteenth century by John Sedding as 'traditional' topiary figures. Using herbs for their scent as well as their shape was a distinctive part of early English topiary, as it had been for knot gardens and mazes. In the last part of the sixteenth century, Barnaby Goodge recorded women trimming and shaping rosemary plants into forms including peacocks, carts or 'such things as they fancy'.

Topiary pieces were known and admired in high status gardens such as Hampton Court, where in 1592 the Duke of Wurzburg admired pieces 'trained, inter-twined and trimmed in so wonderful a fashion and in such extraordinary shapes that the like could not easily be found'. In her book *English Topiary Gardens*, Ethne Clarke records that in 1599 a German traveller noted centaurs, servants with baskets, and figures of men and women at Hampton Court. At Kew, later to become the Royal Botanic Gardens, the Capel family kept their yew hedges in 'pretty shape' with clippers. William Lawson, in his *A New Orchard and Garden* with *The Country Housewife's Garden*', confidently declares that 'Your gardener can frame your lesser wood to the shape of men armed in the field, ready to give battle; of swift running

Opposite:
Detail of a picture of the gardens at Hesse, Germany, in 1631 with trellis hedges similar to those portrayed in Gervase Markham's *The Country Farm.*

'Beasts and Birds' such as rampant lions, or the more humble pig, have an enduring appeal for the topiarist. This box pig was part of the topiary gardens at Compton Wynyates at the beginning of the twentieth century.

greyhounds, or of well scented and true running hounds to chase the deer or hunt the hare. This kind of hunting shall not waste your corn, nor much, your coney'. (Coney was the common word for rabbits.) Another seventeenth-century poet described his vision of the perfect garden: 'Of rosemary, cut out with curious order, in satyrs, centaurs, whale and half-men-horses and a thousand other counterfeited courses.' A Welsh poet records that a fellow bard, Huw Machno, had been commemorated by being cut in topiary in the gardens at Gwydir, Caernarfonshire in Wales. For those with less ambitious or less skilled gardeners, Lawson suggests that plain clipped 'Mazes well framed a man's height, may perhaps make your friend wander in gathering of berries till he cannot recover himself without your help'. Lawson included an illustration of the ideal garden and orchard within his book, showing an armed man and horse in topiary in one of the garden 'compartments' and a complex garden knot in another. The topiary was to be set within fruit orchards ornamenting the spaces within the trees and in the borders and fences. Echoes of Lawson's drawing of a topiary man armed with a sword are found within John Parkinson's *Paradisi in Sole Paradisus Terrestris* (the first three words being a pun on his own name). Dedicated to Queen Elizabeth, this 1629 work describes the cultivation and laying out of gardens, including horticultural techniques. Parkinson referred to the use of both the yew and the privet for ornament. The privet he considered was rather neglected, and he recommends it 'to make hedges or arbours in gardens ... it is so apt that no other can be like unto it, to be cut, lead and drawn into what forme one will either of beasts, birds, or men armed or otherwise'.

Also departing from the use of herbs and evergreens, Gervase Markham suggested that gardeners and estate owners might grow whitethorn, eglantine and sweetsbriar up trelliswork to create clipped forms. Markham's *The Country Farm*, printed in 1615, is the first English book of garden instruction

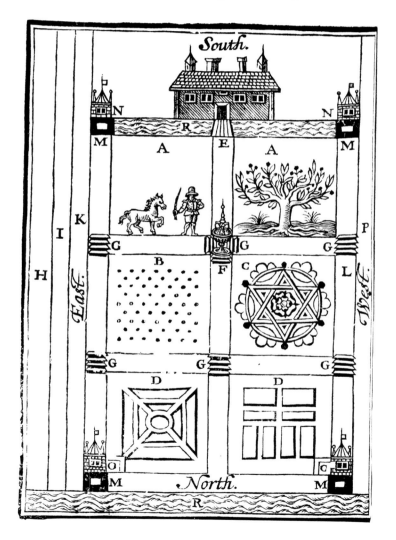

Part of Lawson's (1618) plan of a garden, showing the topiary horse and rider. A Tudor knot is also shown in one of the garden compartments, and might be made of clipped herbs.

specifically to include the creation of topiary. In it there are references to fine and curious hedges 'made battlement-wise in sundrie forms, according to the invention, carrying the proportions of Pyllasters [pilasters], shapes of beasts, birds, creeping things, shippes, trees and such like.' Markham borrowed heavily from French works for his book, but it indicates the knowledge and probable presence of such features in English gardens. The framework for the hedges was to be made of osiers (willow) and wire. These hedges were a popular cross between the palisade hedge and topiary forms.

John Evelyn (the diarist and horticultural writer) claimed to be the first in England to use yews instead of cypress for topiary. Hedges, cones, spires, bowls, and 'what other shapes' were made by him in yew. Evelyn also used holly, and created a famous holly hedge 400 feet long, 9 feet high and 5 feet thick. Evelyn's hedge at Sayes Court (Deptford) was later ruined by Peter the Great when he rented the property. The Tsar of Russia enlivened his leisure moments by being wheeled through the hedge in a wheelbarrow, causing gaps in the magnificent structure. Evelyn also shaped holly into columns and pilasters, 'the berry adorning the inter-columniations with scarlet festoons' and complementing 'four large round phillyreas, smooth clipped and raised on single stalk from the ground'.

Not everybody loved topiary, even in the seventeenth century. Francis Bacon, who wrote the famous essay *Of Gardens* in around 1625, said that,

Suggestions for a trellis fence or hedge with wooden forms on top which could be used to shape hedging from Gervase Markham's *The Country Farm* (1615).

whilst small hedges 'round like welts' and pretty pyramids were allowable, images cut in juniper or other 'garden stuff' were only fit for children. Bacon was unusual in his restrained tastes. Travelling the country houses and gardens of England between 1685 and 1698, Celia Fiennes saw many examples of the topiarist's art. She was fond of the 'old-fashioned' taste and notes approvingly gardens composed of gravel walks, arbours and grass *parterres*. At 'Mr Ruth's House' in Epsom she noted that there were 'dwarf trees of fruit and flowers and greens in all shapes', as well as painted sticks with gilt tops in the greens and flower pots. Also in Epsom, Sir Thomas Cookes's garden included 'two large grass plots beset with green cyprus yew and holly in pyramids', 'the wall clothed with box, holly, phillyrea cut even', whilst Mrs Steeven had '[ever] greens cut in every shape as well as orange and lemon trees and more dwarf fruits'. At Hampton Court, then the new home of King William and Queen Mary, the more restrained 'Dutch' style triumphed by 1698, with cone and balls decorating the *parterres*.

Levens Hall, the famous topiary garden in South Cumbria, is believed to have been first designed and created in 1694. The designer was Guillaume Beaumont, French by origin but possibly by then a religious refugee from Holland, who was the gardener to Colonel James Grahme. Variously credited with working at Hampton Court and even Versailles, Beaumont was to oversee the final 'flowering' of topiary before the introduction of the

The gardens at Hampton Court were recreated in the 1990s and the topiary cones and balls are now established.

Levens Hall as depicted on a postcard of the early twentieth century.

An Edwardian view towards the Gardener's Cottage at Levens Hall.

Hampton Court Palace maze from an early postcard.

informal England landscape garden. Levens Hall is one of the few gardens that largely escaped destruction by this landscape movement and, although substantially restored in the Victorian period, some of the topiary plants there are said to have originated in the seventeenth century. Each of the topiary pieces has a distinctive style and many are named, including the Judge's Wig, Jug of Morocco (a potent drink), Queen Elizabeth and her Maids of Honour, the Lion, etc.

The leading nurserymen of the day, George London and Henry Wise, stocked their Brompton nurseries with evergreens of all shapes and sizes. They recommended bay, pyracanthus, *Arbutus unedo*, *Prunus laurocerasus* and all types of *Phillyrea*, as well as box and yew. In 1712 a Mr Lambert wrote that 'the gardeners about London were remarkable for fine cut greens and clipt yews in the shapes of birds, dogs, men, ships, etc.' Faced with a royal command to beautify a disused gravel pit in Kensington Gardens, royal gardeners created for William III a mimic fortification made in yew and variegated holly with bastions, crenellations and counterscarps all in clipped 'verdure'. Within twenty years topiary would be as much under attack as any real fortification.

Back at Hampton Court, recent research now dates the famous maze to the reign of Queen Anne in *c.* 1714, notable otherwise for her intense dislike of clipped box. The maze originally formed part of a 'wilderness' area, the rest of which had been commissioned by Charles II's mistress, Barbara Villiers, in the 1670s. It may well have been laid out by the same George Beaumont who was later to design Levens Hall, who was at that time living in Richmond. At time of construction the maze was described as 'a hedgework of large evergreens', the plants for which were provided by the nurseryman Henry Wise.

The Stoke Edith Tapestry depicts an upper-class garden of the last years of the seventeenth century, complete with clipped oranges in pots and cone and ball topiary.

SATIRE AND SCORN: THE EIGHTEENTH CENTURY

Those who are on true improvements bent, Must with natural products be content

Sir John Clark of Penicuik, The Country Seat, *1731.*

THE FIRST DECADES of the eighteenth century saw the beginning of the end for the formal garden, and with it the popularity of topiary. Leading the clarion cry for liberation from the niceties of artificial effects and 'curiosities of art' was Joseph Addison (1672–1719). Writing in *The Spectator* in June 1712, Addison decried the fashion for 'Trees [that] rise in Cones, Globes and Pyramids'. The 'Marks of Scissars upon every Plant and Bush' were not to Addison's taste; instead he preferred to look upon 'a Tree in all its Luxuriancy and Diffusion of Boughs and Branches, than when it is thus cut and trimmed into a Mathematical Figure.' Addison blamed nurserymen such as George London and Henry Wise for promoting this outmoded and ridiculous fashion for the sake of their own profits. As a contemporary commented: 'As our great modellers of gardens have their magazines of plants to dispose of, it is very natural for them to tear up all the beautiful plantations and contrive a plan that may most turn to their own profit'.

Stephen Switzer's book on garden and landscape design, published in 1715 under the all-encompassing title *The Nobleman, Gentleman and Gardener's Recreation*, followed Addison's grand views on opening up the landscape to nature, although the book's frontispiece showed a formal *parterre* garden replete with cone and ball topiary in pots. By 1742 Switzer (1682–1745) was declaring that 'a Design must submit to Nature and not Nature to his Design', and the very title of his later book *Iconographia Rustica* eschewed artifice. Even the primacy of the classical taste was called into question when it was declared by Robert Castell in his *Villas of the Ancients* (1728) that 'it cannot be supposed that Nature ever did or ever will produce Trees in the form of beasts, or letters or any resemblance of embroidery … which appear monstrous'. Even the architect of Pliny's villa, Castell suggests, 'knew better, but had been induced by the gardeners to make use of these ornaments'!

Although the ancients might have been 'induced' to formality, few in eighteenth-century England would be brave enough to stand against the tide of fashion. Writing in the *Guardian*, Alexander Pope, garden enthusiast, classicist and arbiter of taste, argued that the 'amiable simplicity of Nature' and not the 'nicer scenes of art' had been the true classical taste. In Pope's own garden at Twickenham, there was no 'shear work', and the holly, laurel, bay and other evergreens grew as nature intended, disporting uncontrolled. According to Pope, only people of the 'common level' could possibly like trees in the awkward figures of men and animals, whilst the loftier mind must always turn to unadorned nature. Menials such as cooks created topiary coronation dinners, with the queen in perpetual green youth. 'A Citizen',
declared Pope, 'is no sooner proprietor of a couple of yews, but he entertains thoughts of erecting them into giants'. To 'assist' those who had this low taste, Pope produced a catalogue of topiary supposedly being marketed by an eminent nurseryman. The catalogue of course is fiction, and contains several levels of jest – both in the mockery it makes of topiary figures and its historical and political asides. 'Queen Elizabeth I cut in myrtle, a little forward but miscarried through being too near a savine' was presumed to be a reference to Queen Elizabeth's supposed love affair with Robert Dudley, savine being used as a herbal abortifacient. An 'Old Maid on Wormwood' was a reference to the supposed bitterness of both the shrub itself and unmarried women.

George still not quite in a condition to 'stick the dragon'! This George, next to Doncaster Cathedral, is technically mosaiculture rather than topiary.

Other items on the list by Alexander Pope included:

> ADAM and Eve in yew; Adam a little shatter'd by the fall of the Tree of
>   knowledge in the great storm; Eve and the Serpent very flourishing.
> THE Tower of Babel, not yet finished.
> ST GEORGE in box; his arm scarce long enough, but will be in a
>   condition to stick the Dragon by next April.
> A Green Dragon of the same, with a Tail of Ground Ivy for the present.
>   N.B. These two not to be sold separately.
> EDWARD The Black Prince in Cypress.
> A Laurustine BEAR in Blossom, with a Juniper Hunter in Berries;
> A topping Ben Johnson in Laurel.
> DIVERSE eminent Modern Poets in Bays, somewhat blighted, to be
>   disposed of a pennyworth.
> A Quick-set Hog shot up into a Porcupine by its being forgot a week in
>   rainy weather.
> A Lavender Pig with Sage growing in his Belly.

Topiary pigs
(of box rather
than lavender).

In his guide to all that was tasteful in gardening, Batty Langley's *New Principles of Gardening* (1728) argued that:

I cannot well conclude this section without taking notice of those wretched Figures many Nursery-Men and Gardeners breed up their Hollies and Ever-Greens in, as the forms of men on horseback, as against Hyde Park Gate by Kensington; when they know no more of the Anatomy or Proportion of those Figures, than they do of the beautiful proportions of Architecture, which they ignorantly attempt to execute, when they breed up Yews, Hollies etc in the forms of Ballustrades, pedestals etc with the most deformed body plac'd thereon, by them called a round or a square column, which hath neither Base, Shaft, nor Capital, or indeed any one thing in them as is beautiful or pleasing. And seeing that our British Nation does at this time consist of the most Noble Grand Planters and Encouragers of Gardening of any in Europe tis to be hoped that, for the future, better rules will be observed therein, that is, such as are consistent with reason, Art, nature and that such Plants as have received such former Injuries, may be restored to their proper and Natural Shapes as soon as Time can operate the same.

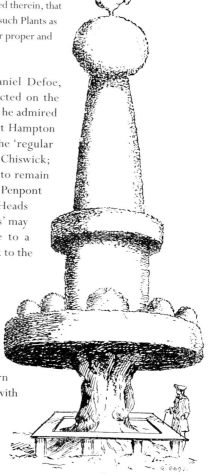

The Harlington Oak was a rare example of topiary that survived through the eighteenth century, being recorded as clipped into this specific shape from 1729–90.

Few stood out for long against this naturalism. Daniel Defoe, touring England in 1724–6 and again in 1742, reflected on the changes in fashion for topiary and clipped box. In 1724 he admired the 'fair and regular' box hedges of the royal garden at Hampton Court, but by 1742 he comments disparagingly on the 'regular walks with clipped hedges on each side' still in place at Chiswick; 'it is to be wondered his Lordship should suffer them to remain in the present form'. In 1775 a visitor to the gardens at Penpont in Wales noted 'two foolish Yew Lions, with wooden Heads thrust into the top of them, that stare at you'. The 'heads' may have been formers not yet covered, or a reference to a combined piece of topiary/sculpture work harking back to the Roman and Renaissance styles.

When Lord Perceval, 1st Earl of Egmont (1683–1748) visited Hall Barn, Buckinghamshire, in 1724 he was still able to record that there were 'several apartments, arches, corridors, etc, composed of high thriving, Yews, cut very artfully'. The gardens with their statues, terraces and gravelled walks reminded Lord Perceval of Versailles, but unlike Versailles the gardens at Hall Barn were in the process of being softened into an English style with winding walks, ha-has and the inclusion of the distant rural landscape in the views. The topiary was doomed. In France the Revolution was not to begin until 1789, but in England the landscape revolution at least was already under way by the early eighteenth century.

SNEERS AND SHEARS: THE VICTORIAN TOPIARY DEBATE

The man who sneers at me for admiring, as I do, a well cut peacock, may take my assurance in advance that I will neither kick him nor abuse him; but pity him I must.

James Shirley Hibberd quoted in Curtis's The Book of Topiary *(1904).*

A stone, hewn into a graceful ornamented vase or urn, has a value which it did not before possess, a yew hedge clipped, is only defaced. The one is a production of art, the other a distortion of nature.

Sir Walter Scott (1771–1832)

Aesthetically ideal for the formality of the Victorian bedding system, topiary was nevertheless often scorned for its lack of refinement and taste and ridiculed for its 'old-fashioned' style during much of the nineteenth century. This ambivalence on the part of the arbiters of taste did not prevent horticulturalists such as William Barron, head gardener at Elvaston Castle, Derbyshire, creating massive clipped hedges and specimen pieces. Barron spent almost twenty years (1830–50) working for the fourth Earl of Petersham, creating 'instant' gardens of mature trees for his reclusive employer and his much younger actress wife, whom he kept in complete seclusion. The mysterious gardens became so famous that when they were finally opened to the public on the death of the earl in 1851, thousands flocked to see them, and the yew avenues and specimen pieces caused a sensation.

By the middle of the nineteenth century, horticultural writers were beginning to look more kindly on topiary. In his popular book *The Suburban Gardener and Villa Companion,* published in 1838, John Claudius Loudon stated that:

> where no other artistical or curious mineral, or sculptural object, is introduced, an evergreen shrub, such as a privet, a juniper, or a yew, may be cut into the shape of some artistical object; as at Hendon, where, in the front garden of one of the houses in the village, there are two Louis XIVth vases in box.

Opposite:
Elvaston Castle topiary gardens as they appeared at the time of public opening in the 1850s.

33

Loudon's rival and successor, (James) Shirley Hibberd, took a rather more emotive and moralising approach to gardening than Loudon. Writing in the 1860s, he declared that:

> I confess that I should never care to adorn my garden with topiary or with carpet bedding; but I hope always to be cautious in making declarations in respect of such matters, that I may not appear to despise another man's pleasures, or vainly desire to set up a standard of my own in opposition to the delightful variety that is ensured by the free exercise of individual taste and fancy.

Like many a garden writer, Hibberd could obviously admire a well-clipped evergreen without necessarily wanting one in his own garden! Despite this rather forgiving approach by the foremost garden writer of the period, the popular Thompson's *Gardener's Assistant* published in 1859 did not include any mention of topiary in its instructions on all things needful for the kitchen, fruit and flower garden.

After this brief renaissance, by the 1870s the gardening public was being urged to turn away from formal planting and bedding towards the more informal plantings that would eventually be known as the 'English Flower Garden' style. The main proponent of that style was William Robinson, an immensely knowledgeable but rather irascible writer whose influence was to loom down the years via his protégé Gertrude Jekyll. In 1883 Robinson published *The English Flower Garden*. Enormously popular, this was to be continually re-printed and re-published through fifteen editions. With each edition Robinson grew more violent against the clipping of trees, the main trigger point being his public clash with the formal landscape architects Sir Reginald Blomfield and John Sedding in 1892 and later with distinguished writers such as Nathaniel Lloyd.

A specimen yew combining seat and peacocks at Elvaston.

Sedding, writing in the provocatively named (to Robinson) *Garden Craft Old and New* in 1891, had suggested that 'There is a quaint charm in the results of topiary art, in the prim imagery of evergreens', and

> I would even introduce *bizarreries* on the principle of not leaving all that is wild and odd to nature; and in the formal part of the garden my yews should take the shape of pyramids, or peacocks or cocked hats or ramping lions or any other conceit I had a mind to.

These massive tiered yews, shown here in 1870, were contemporary with the writings of James Shirley Hibberd, a popular garden writer whose works appealed to suburban and cottage garden owners.

The following year (1892), Blomfield, architect and landscape designer, also published a work which promoted the 'old-fashioned' or formal garden replete with arbours, alleys, and topiary specimens. With illustrations of formal gardens such as Montacute (Somerset), Canons Ashby (Northamptonshire), Risley (Derbyshire), Levens Hall (Westmorland) and the formal yew walk at Melbourne (Derbyshire), and quotations from seventeenth- and eighteenth-century garden writers, Blomfield championed the old symmetrical, clipped garden.

Robinson, on the other hand, claimed that deforming of trees, most especially the noble yew, was an abortion rather than an art. Under the heading 'Misuse of the Yew Tree in Gardens', Robinson decried everything about topiary, from the early death of plants due to their close planting, to the waste of time spent clipping those few plants that did survive! Mazes were dismissed as monstrosities, seats and other forms were 'absurd', and clipped hedges were just so many dead lines. Taking exception to the recent increase in articles and pictures of topiary in the magazine *Country Life*, Robinson declared that its pages contained some of the 'worst forms of distortion of our forest evergreen tree'. Yew, holly, arbutus and box were, to Robinson, things of native beauty best left to grow in their 'wild' shapes. Non-native evergreens were on the other hand dismissed as 'ugly' and 'monstrous' even when not clipped. Gardeners incapable of appreciating the natural forms were dismissed as dead to beauty of form, callous and foolish. Memorably coining the phrase 'A gardener with shears in his hand is generally doing fool's work', Robinson fulminated against all magazines, journals, writers and gardeners who dared to trim their evergreens.

Cheerful birds and beasts in yew, such as this sleepy pig and fox at Wenlock Priory, would be anathema to William Robinson.

Levens Hall pictured at the period Blomfield was writing in praise of the topiary there.

Given Robinson's uncompromising position, it was not surprising that he referred (in his later editions) to Nathaniel Lloyd's *Garden Craftsmanship in Yew and Box* (1925) as 'the poorest book that has ever disfigured the garden', producing feelings of vexation and then pity. We will return to Nathaniel Lloyd later.

Despite his support for William Robinson over 'hideous' garden design elements such as carpet bedding, the leading Arts and Crafts designer, William Morris, approved of both the 'Old World' garden and of topiary figures, as did garden designer Gertrude Jekyll, who was also part of the Arts and Crafts movement. For Morris, topiary combined the art of clipping with the craft of gardens (a term notably coined in John Sedding's 1891 book *Garden Craft Old and New*). Sedding was much admired by Morris and other members of the Arts and Crafts movement, and was a member of the Art Workers' Guild. Sedding's book included numerous illustrations where statues, *parterres*, and flowers were complemented by box hedging and topiary figures to create the quintessential Old World garden beloved of the Morris school. On the other hand, the influential art critic and social thinker John Ruskin (1819–1900) felt that 'the custom of clipping trees into fantastic forms is always to be reprehended'.

LEVENS GARDENS.

Compton Wynyates was famous for its topiary gardens in the early twentieth century.

The gardens at Owlpen, Gloucestershire, are typical of the Arts and Crafts Movement, combining tall clipped hedges, topiary shapes and overflowing borders.

An illustration from John Sedding's *Garden Craft Old and New* (1891).

VOL. XVIII. HANDBOOKS OF
PRACTICAL GARDENING

THE BOOK OF
TOPIARY

BY

CHARLES H. CURTIS,
& W. GIBSON.

CHESSMEN AND PEACOCKS:
EDWARDIAN DELIGHTS

WRITING in 1904, Charles Curtis commented regretfully that his newly published book on topiary was 'not placed before the public with any fervent hope that it will incite garden lovers to at once sally forth with shears and scissors', nor was it published to supply 'a long felt want'; rather it was 'produced to provide an hour's reading in one of the most distinct and interesting branches of horticulture that the art has ever produced'. Most other practical garden works published in the period tended either to ignore topiary or to decry it as an outmoded fashion, one belonging more to the distant Tudor age than the modern times of the new century. Written in partnership with W. Gibson, head gardener at the famous Levens Hall, Charles Curtis' *The Book of Topiary* unexpectedly sparked a revival. Illustrated with images of the few mature gardens that still contained topiary collections, the book gave practical instructions on training and managing topiary figures and photographs of topiary 'in the making'.

Also in *The Book of Topiary* were photographs of specimens being grown in the nurseries of the period, including those at the Cheal nurseries. J. Cheal and Sons (Crawley) had been growing and exhibiting topiary from at least 1899. *The Gardeners' Chronicle* review of the famous Temple Exhibition of that year included the following note:

> Messrs J CHEAL & Sons, Lowfield Nuseries, Crawley, had also rhododendrons, Azaleas, and a topiary exhibit of Box and Yew Trees, a revival of an old-fashioned fancy which we cherish when old, but deprecate when new…

In the same year *The Gardeners' Chronicle* reported from the Royal Horticultural Show that:

> much interest centred upon Messrs Cheal's exhibit of quite the newest of gardening revivals in the taste that is springing up afresh for the yew and box bushes, clipped in the Old Dutch fashion. It is only in a very few old

Opposite:
Curtis & Gibson's
The Book of Topiary,
published 1904.

world gardens that these are still to be found, but here were shown some of
the quaintest forms that were favoured of yore in spirals, hens and peacocks.

By the following year *The Gardeners' Chronicle* had changed its opinions and
wrote a very 'cutting' piece calling the topiary pieces 'vegetable
monstrosities', regarded only by those 'gentlemen' who wanted instant
gardens. Torn between praising the nurserymen they represented and
insulting the fashion for topiary, the editors of the *Chronicle* stated:

> If we are careful to first point out that any word of praise we can give such
> exhibits must be wholly from the point of view of the 'trainer', then the
> extensive and very remarkable collection shown by Messrs CUTBUSH and
> Sons, Highgate, and the smaller group from Messrs CHEAL, were worthy
> of remark. Some of the specimens, whether they mimicked a peacock, a
> boat, a monkey or a sheep, or a table with wineglasses, bore such evident
> indication of skillful and painstaking work, that as objects of skillful but ill-
> advised effort they were excellent.

The Cheal nurseries, captured in photographs of the period, had a veritable
army of box peacocks of all heights and sizes. Lined up as if in some gigantic
chess game composed of hundreds of pieces, rows of spirals give way to first
balls, then cones, then peacocks. Peacocks were the most imperial of birds and
popular in aristocratic houses, but Cheals also sold the more humble hens and
ducks – usually in box rather than the more aristocratic yew. Between 1903
and 1908 Lord Astor employed Cheals' topiary expert, Peter Breden, to create
the famous Henry VIII chessmen in 'Ann Boleyn's' garden at Hever Castle in

The topiary section at Cheal's nursery c. 1920.

A display of topiary at the Chelsea Flower Show in 2009 is reminiscent of the displays by Cheals at the Temple Shows in 1899 and 1900.

Kent, basing his clipped shapes on records in the British Museum. Cheals also supplied the one thousand, six-foot-tall, yew plants for Hever's famous maze. In 1914 Cheals were honoured with a Victoria Medal of Honour by the Royal Horticultural Society, with especial reference to their 'promotion of topiary', despite anything *The Gardeners' Chronicle* thought!

Another important topiary supplier of the period was the rather serendipitously named Wm. Cutbush & Son of Highgate. Mr Herbert Cutbush frequently travelled to Holland to examine specimens of topiary work, not just in the nurseries of that country but also in private gardens. Discovering that some of the best examples of topiary work were to be found in the small farmhouse gardens, well away from the tourist trails, he laid claim to

Right:
Klinkert nurseries
were also
a veritable
cornucopia of
clipped shapes.

CUTBUSH'S
"CUT BUSHES"

A very fine collection of Box and Yew cut into
many quaint forms.
A nice lot of Pyramid and Ball Shaped Box
suitable for tubs and vases.
List Post Free.
Can be inspected at our Barnet Nurseries.

Wm. Cutbush & Son, Ltd.,
Nurserymen by Appointment to His Majesty the King.

Barnet   Nurseries,   Barnet,   Herts.

Telephone : BARNET 2.

THE KEW TOPIARY NURSERIES LTD.
(formerly JOHN KLINKERT, F.R.H.S.)
STANMORE ROAD, RICHMOND, SURREY
Telephone: RIChmond 0550

•

¶ Come and visit our Topiary Nurseries (pictured overleaf) and
see for yourself nearly 10,000 pieces in all stages of growth.

¶ You will see also many wonderful and very scarce Specimen
Trees — in Box and Yew — from 25 to 75 years old, which
cannot be seen elsewhere.

¶ After your visit you can cross the road into Kew Gardens, an
afternoon well spent.

¶ The Nursery is situated in Stanmore Road, just off Kew Road,
about 150 yards from the Lion Gate, Kew Gardens.

An advertisement for the wonderfully aptly named
Wm. Cutbush & Son nurseries.

An advertisement for the new 'Kew Topiary
Nurseries'. Note the use of the wooden formers.

Another view of the Klinkert nurseries.

The topiary gardens at Friar Park, pictured in c. 1900. Sir Frank Crisp at Friar Park, Oxfordshire, was amongst the first to create a garden in the new topiary fashion.

The complicated topiary gardens at Hewell Grange, Worcestershire, where arches predominated rather than figures, c. 1907.

A postcard of
Great Dixter
(Sussex), c. 1925.

ENHANCE THE BEAUTY OF YOUR GARDEN

MORE and more keen amateur gardeners are relying on topiary for that "professional" effect—that finishing touch. Perhaps your problem demands just such a solution. That path intersection; that bare space in the porch; a dozen positions instantly present themselves as appropriate for one or other of these attractively trimmed Box Trees.

We have fifteen thousand to select from, and they vary in age from ten to forty years. They grow very slowly but live for more than a hundred years, requiring but little attention.

★
Write for price list and range of shapes in Box Trees and Yew Trees, or better still, call and inspect these beautiful designs.

It is difficult to imagine a more permanent contribution to the beauty of your garden than one or more of these fine examples of the Topiarist's Art.

JOHN KLINKERT F.R.H.S.
Established 1907   *Telephone : Richmond 0550*
KEW TOPIARY NURSERIES RICHMOND SURREY

WHEN REPLYING TO ADVERTISERS

iv

GARDEN DESIGN

A QUARTERLY JOURNAL OF HORTICULTURE & GARDEN ARCHITECTURE

PRICE ONE SHILLING   No. 34 SUMMER 1938

Books such as Nathaniel Lloyd's gave impetus to the inter-war fashion and topiary nurseries expanded.

The topiary peacocks at Great Dixter sparked renewed interest in this particular topiary form, shown here on the cover of a fashionable 'garden architect' periodical.

The Last Supper was one of the more complex scenes in topiary and needed to be grown in situ. Most gardens preferred smaller pieces that were available direct from the nurseries.

Topiary sundials with yew 'gnomen' appear to have been an Edwardian innovation, shown here at Stainborough, South Yorkshire.

promising specimens. On one occasion he claimed to have spent an entire day negotiating for a particularly aged specimen that had for sixty years decorated a blacksmith's garden. At last succeeding in gaining his prize, he spent a further week lifting and packing it for the London market. In addition he traded with the 'Boomkmeckers', Dutch nurserymen based around the Boskoop district who cultivated clipped trees. The shapes that could be acquired in Holland were even more variable than those popular in England. Hens, ducks, geese and dogs were joined by tables, chairs, armchairs and even churches! Sailing ships and barges were much prized, but difficult to train and maintain.

By 1910 the fashion for topiary gardens, as well as individual specimens, was well established. Topiary gardens were created at Ascot (Berks) for Leopold Rothschild, for Lady Dudley at Witley Court (Worcestershire – destroyed by fire in 1937), at Hewell Grange (Worcestershire), at Hever Castle (Kent) and for Mr

In 1938 the Klinkert nurseries were already overstocked. By the end of following year most nurseries would be forced to divert their energies to productive plants.

R. Hudson at Danesfield (Marlow, Bucks). There were also gardens where topiary appeared to have survived from the eighteenth or even seventeenth century into the Edwardian era, and these were held up as ideals of the old-fashioned garden. Amongst the most famous of these was Levens Hall (Westmorland). However, claims for such longevity might be greeted with some skepticism, as both individual plants and their original shapes might have varied, even if the overall appearance of the garden had not. W. Gibson, head gardener at Levens Hall, commented in Curtis' *The Book of Topiary* that ' A record of the date of planting and the shapes that the trees were originally meant to represent, seems to have been a thing quite neglected during the formation of the old topiary gardens, which seems to me a very great pity'.

Edwardian topiary gardens could take many forms. Sunken gardens, where the topiary forms could be admired from adjoining terraces, were a favourite. Compartmentalised gardens with buttresses and hedges provided ideal shelter for specimens and the hedges were also clipped, providing a formal setting for the actual topiary. Laying out the garden in a series of squares or rectangles allowed patterns to be repeated or varied within a formal structure. Rather incongruent in this picture of decorative formality, Curtis suggested that any areas within the hedges not taken up by topiary might form a vegetable and fruit garden. Yew, including golden yew, and box were preferred, with holly being considered too messy.

In 1925 Nathaniel Lloyd published what became the topiarist's handbook. Entitled *Garden Craftsmanship in Yew and Box*, this well-illustrated manual combining history with cultivation techniques was to inspire the inter-war fashion for the placement of birds on cones and pillars, tunnels and precisely battered hedges. Spirit levels, flat-capped gardeners, battens and string were an essential to these immaculately manicured avenues and arches. Nathaniel Lloyd had been creating the gardens and topiary at Great Dixter (Sussex) since 1912 and gave advice on planting and moving of yew trees based on his own experience. Photographs of his own planting at Great Dixter can be compared with the same topiary hedges and pieces now at these famous gardens.

A far wider range of shapes was instantly available to early twentieth-century topiarists than to their earlier counterparts, whilst the range of evergreens had also increased substantially. As well as birds and beasts, letters of the alphabet had made a comeback from the Roman period. Instructions on making the letters 'A' and 'B' were contained within Curtis and Gibson's *The Book of Topiary*, and a famous 'B' was trained in the gardens of Levens Hall. If the topiarist tired of alphabets there were barrister's wigs, Indian wigwams, summerhouses, helmets, busbys, bottles, umbrellas, hats, chairs, etc. In addition a larger garden might hold a 'scene' such as a dining table and diners, chessmen, The Last Supper, or Adam and Eve in Eden. Curtis recommended that at least five different shapes of topiary arch be employed in any topiary garden, with few things being more effective than a well-trained arch. For the less skilled it was a relief to know that 'There are a great many very pretty shapes that can be formed out of the yew or boxwood tree without being intended to represent anything in particular'.

The cost of ready-made topiary pieces meant that these were mostly reserved for high-status gardens. In the inter-war period, topiary birds might vary from 3 guineas to 10 guineas depending on age, size and condition. Yew, being slower to grow than box, was invariably more expensive, with large birds taking anything between 20 and 60 years to grow. Even box might take 10–12 years for a small bird, with tall designs in tiers or pillars taking 15–18 years. Of course if you were a patient gardener than you could plant and grow your own topiary pieces, carefully watching them develop over the decades, a tweak here, a prune there. But for many, when the fashion hit, buying in was the only way left open.

In 1934 the Klinkert nursery exhibited 'An Old World Topiary Garden' at the Ideal Home Exhibition, and in 1937 it displayed a garden entitled 'Dante and Beatrice'. Klinkert's later became 'The Kew Topiary Nursery', situated in Stanmore Rd, still providing plants from 25 to 75 years of age, all lovingly hand formed – many using wooden forms or guides. By 1938, with the worry of war looming, they were trying to sell excess stock of topiary plants.

The topiary sundial at the Gardens of Easton Lodge, Essex. The original sundial was created as part of the private gardens of Daisy, Duchess of Warwick, in the early twentieth century and was recreated in 2000.

TEAPOTS AND CATS: COTTAGE GARDEN TOPIARY

Aᴸᴛʜᴏᴜɢʜ its origins had been the royal and aristocratic garden, topiary also found a home in small gardens. During the late nineteenth and early twentieth centuries, 'cottage garden' topiary became famous in its own right, with postcards published of particularly famous sites. Most cottage gardens had just one or two pieces, as befitted their size. Teapots, 'cake-stands', and cats were popular, with the occasional peacock, often looking slightly more rotund and less regal in their rural backdrop. Lovingly tended, many pieces eventually towered over the cottages they sat next to, creating a Lilliputian effect. Individual pieces might become famous if they were on popular tourist routes. The village of Broadway in the Cotswolds, for example, is on a walking tour that leads to the prehistoric burial chamber of Belas Knapp. Along the Knapp road was a much-photographed cottage with topiary, and the churchyard of the village also boasted clipped work.

Yew or box were most likely to be used in cottage gardens, giving rise to endless 'Yew Tree Cottages', with other shrubs more difficult to get hold of or needing more care and attention, although in the twentieth century euonymus was a popular alternative, giving extra colour in its variegated form.

Some cottage gardeners were more ambitious, and the sheer scale and intricacies of scenic groups testified to the amateur's fascination with this 'verdant art'. One of the most famous cottage topiary gardens was that at Glyn Aur, Abergwili (Carmarthenshire). The gardens (situated on the wonderfully named Castell Pigyn Road) were created in the early twentieth century by the owner of the cottage, Mr D. Davies. Mr Davies was a photographer and published many postcards of the evergreen religious scenes he had created. After his death the garden was kept up by Mr Davies's son, but is now sadly lost.

The association with the Arts and Crafts Movement made cottage garden topiary, at least

Opposite:
This delightful watercolour by the noted artist Thomas Hunn captures the idealised country cottage garden with its rambling flowers and old world topiary. Painted at Old Basing in 1918, it depicts a world about to disappear for ever.

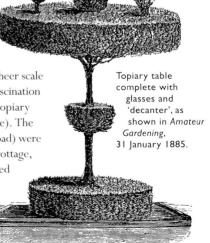

Topiary table complete with glasses and 'decanter', as shown in *Amateur Gardening*, 31 January 1885.

The topiary 'Flight to Egypt' at Glyn Aur, Abergwili.

Another religiously inspired topiary scene at Glyn Aur. The 'crucifixion' is an unusual topiary scene.

Like at Glyn Aur, the residents in this cottage at Herstmonceux (Sussex) used a combination of training and topiary to declare their religious beliefs.

Topiary in the
cottage garden
on the Knapp
road, Broadway,
Cotswolds, c. 1912.

This strange
coffee pot/teapot
combination is
a type popular in
cottage gardens.
Here it sits rather
oddly in the
gardens at
Glendoune
Mansion House,
c. 1907.

Cottage topiary is alive and well in the twenty-first century, albeit less orthodox!

Another teapot, this time appropriately in Mrs West's Tea Garden in Surrey (1909).

the more traditional forms of individual peacocks, cats, etc., a suitable subject for romantic rural watercolours and postcards. The association with supposedly timeless tradition, careful industry and quiet pride amongst the rural labouring classes made such images favourites alongside watercolours by artists such as Helen Allingham and Beatrice Parsons.

REDISCOVERING TOPIARY

GARDEN FASHION is fickle, and as had happened in the eighteenth century, so the mid-twentieth century again saw a decline in the popularity of topiary. The Second World War, which had wrought such destruction on gardens and gardeners alike, rang a death knell for labour-intensive gardening everywhere. Nurseries had to clear their stocks to make way for more prosaic vegetables in the Dig for Victory campaign, and gardeners were looking for instant and colourful effects to cheer the austerity years of the 1950s. Formal gardens gave way to an odd mix of urban concrete planning and informal country garden borders. In 1956 Cecil Stewart was driven to remark that:

> Topiary does not belong to our time; it exists only as a relic of an old tradition... Today it is regarded only as something quaint. The idea of carved vegetation no longer fits into our notion of gardening. It belongs, rather, to that looking-glass world in which it was quite the thing for playing-card gardeners to paint the roses red because they had grown up white.

It was the birth of garden history as a discipline that sparked a reawakening of interest in topiary. Historic gardens began to be regarded in the same light as historic houses, places to be protected and possibly restored or recreated. Historic fashions were re-examined, and even large seventeenth-century gardens such as Hampton Court and Versailles were brought back to their original trimmed glory. Tudor, Dutch and Edwardian gardens vied with each other to have their yew hedges and box *parterres* re-planted, and outgrown peacocks had their wings hastily clipped and trimmed to await the rush of visitors to historic gardens. As gardens entered the twenty-first century, topiary was again 're-discovered' by modern garden designers anxious to bring solid shapes and textures back into the design of the garden and the borders. In some instances old topiary features were trimmed and placed amongst new planting, in others entire new designs were created. Amongst the new influences and techniques are hedges cut in 'relief' (ideal for small gardens where a solid hedge is still wanted for privacy, or where a tableau

Topiary 'in relief' is gaining popularity, allowing figures to be cut even in small gardens. This farmyard-themed example is in a small garden near Belton (Lincs).

At East Ruston (Norfolk), the old and new topiary garden styles are combined to give a contrasting feel to different garden areas. Here is a topiary ball border.

Mythical figures have great appeal to modern topiarists, as shown here in a small front garden in Bedford.

effect is wanted), 'cloud topiary' inspired by traditional Japanese clipped work, textured and coloured forms created from multiple species or varieties, and sinuous forms, departing from the traditional formality of flat-tops and straight sides. Allowing part of the plant to 'grow out' or become 'fluffy' also creates a contrast between formal and informal within the same plant. As fashion for topiary in the urban garden grows, single specimens in pots are increasingly popular, although box rarely performs well in pots as it is liable to both drying and water-logging.

In addition to topiary in the garden, topiary pieces now appear within the house in such varied capacities as Christmas decorations, wallpaper, curtain fabrics, place name holders for wedding receptions, and decorative doormats. Taking the desire for slow growth to its logical extremes, artificial topiary that never needs trimming is also now available masquerading as box or yew. It is even possible to buy miniature topiary pieces to decorate the up-market dolls' house, although so far only artificial examples are available!

Based on the Japanese tradition of 'cloud' topiary, this style of topiary is becoming increasingly popular, although very expensive.

Contrasting colours and textures in the topiary at East Ruston.

THE TOPIARIST'S ART

A LTHOUGH topiary can be created from a wide range of herbs, shrubs and even small trees, traditional choices from the seventeenth century onwards concentrated on slow-growing evergreens, usually with small leaves or needles that did not show the mark of the shears. Compact forms hold the clipped shapes better, and fastigiate or columnar varieties can be used to advantage for tiered, pillar or spiral forms.

Images rarely capture the tools of topiary, but this proud householder at Wenlock Edge has been persuaded to pose with his traditional topiary shears.

The most common shrubs that have been used in the past include box (*Buxus sempervirens*), privet (*Ligustrum spp.*), yew (*Taxus spp.*), juniper (*Juniperus*), holly (*Ilex spp.*), myrtle (*Myrtus spp.*), euonymus, Thuja or arborvitae (*Thuja spp.*), phillyrea (also known as mock-privet), and rosemary (*Rosmarinus officinalis*). Bay laurel (*Laurus nobilis*) was also used in the Roman period, but is generally less successful for complex shapes. Cypress and hawthorn are also used for clipped hedging, along with beech, hornbeam and laurustinus (*Viburnum tinus*). Using ivy to grow over wire cages has been defined as a form of topiary, as the ivy is then clipped, but many would see this as lying outside the traditional definition and skating perilously close to 'three dimensional carpet bedding' or mosaiculture. Knot gardens typically utilised a much wider range of plants including santolina, thyme, lavender, rosemary, hyssop, teucrium (germander) and sage. Some of these were really woven rather than clipped into shape, although rosemary and lavender can make successful topiary forms as evidenced by Barnaby

Goodge's reference in the seventeenth century to women weaving shapes out of it.

Yew has a notoriously long lifespan and topiary figures made in yew are often claimed as being original Tudor or Elizabethan specimens. Recently doubt has been cast on these claims by John Glenn, a specialist in yew and box who has concluded that topiary was not usually made of yew until at least the second part of the seventeenth century, whilst 'it is quite possible that there isn't a single authentic example of an ornamental box feature planted before the nineteenth century in the whole country'. Even where a yew might be original the actual topiary design will probably have grown out, or altered and been re-clipped differently over time. The popular *Buxus sempervirens* 'Suffruticosa' may also be a different dwarf box from that recommended in the seventeenth and early eighteenth centuries, making accurate restoration projects difficult. In the mid-seventeenth century, André Mollet in *Le Jardin de Plaisir* described two types of box: the larger wood box which might be allowed to grow naturally, and the small dwarf box which was ideally suited for embroidered *parterres*.

At its most basic, topiary consists of clipping a shrub into a shape; a hedge for example is a form of the topiarist's work. To create more complex shapes, however, the plant must be slowly accustomed to its shaping, with its initial form or general outline introduced early on, otherwise clipping will result

This compact spiral has been created in box.

Regular clipping is essential to maintain shape!

Even the best-tended topiary can seem a little 'fuzzy' just before its annual clipping!

Different clipping regimes can produce some interesting effects, for example here at Lamport Hall (Northants).

in unsightly contrasts between green leaf and bare stalk or stem. Although many of the species used will sprout again readily from branches, others are reluctant to grow from bare wood and will leave unattractive gaps in the greenery if, for example, a rounded bush is suddenly 'transformed' to a pillar or a plump cat to a slim spiral. Slowly but surely is therefore the best motto for the topiarist. Nathaniel Lloyd thought that in the initial creation of a piece *'festina lente'*, or 'make haste slowly', should be the topiarist's motto! Once established the shapes need to be clipped according to the speed of growth, and the slower-growing varieties are most popular.

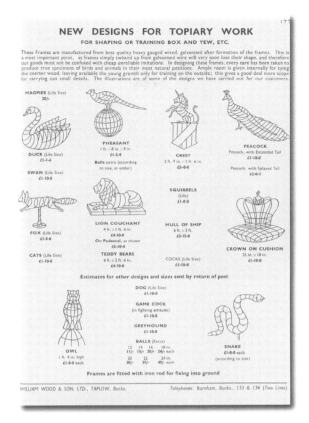

NEW DESIGNS FOR TOPIARY WORK

FOR SHAPING OR TRAINING BOX AND YEW, ETC.

These Frames are manufactured from best quality heavy gauged wired, galvanised after formation of the frames. This is a most important point, as frames simply twisted up from galvanised wire will very soon lose their shape, and therefore our goods must not be confused with cheap unreliable imitations. In designing these frames, every care has been taken to produce true specimens of birds and animals in their most natural positions. Ample room is given internally for tying the coarser wood, leaving available the young growth only for training on the outside; this gives a good deal more scope for carrying out small details. The illustrations are of some of the designs we have carried out for our customers.

MAGPIES (Life Size)
20/-

DUCK (Life Size)
£1-1-6

SWAN (Life Size)
£1-10-0

FOX (Life Size)
£1-5-0

CATS (Life Size)
£1-10-0

PHEASANT
1 ft. × 8 in. × 9 in.
£1-5-0
Balls extra (according to size, as under)

CREST
2 ft. 9 in. × 1 ft. 6 in.
£3-0-0

PEACOCK
Peacock, with Extended Tail
£1-18-0
Peacock, with Splayed Tail
£2-0-0

SQUIRRELS
(Life)
£1-0-0

LION COUCHANT
4 ft. × 1 ft. 6 in.
£4-10-0
On Pedestal, as shown
£5-10-0

HULL OF SHIP
6 ft. × 3 ft.
£3-15-0

CROWN ON CUSHION
21 in. × 18 in.
£1-10-0

TEDDY BEARS
6 ft. × 2 ft. 6 in.
£4-10-0

COCKS (Life Size)
£1-10-0

Estimates for other designs and sizes sent by return of post

DOG (Life Size)
£1-10-0

GAME COCK
(in fighting attitude)
£1-10-0

GREYHOUND
£1-10-0

BALLS (Extra)
12   14   16   18 in.
11/-   15/- 20/- 24/- each
20   22   24 in.
30/-   35/- 45/- each

OWL
1 ft. 4 in. high
£1-0-0 each

SNAKE
£1-0-0 each
(according to size)

Frames are fitted with iron rod for fixing into ground

WILLIAM WOOD & SON. LTD., TAPLOW, Bucks.   Telephones: Burnham, Bucks., 133 & 134 (Two Lines)

Grown on a Euonymus Shrub
by John Ellett
It is now 6 years old.   1919.

Although not as common as the smaller leafed box or the yew, euonymus can make a successful topiary piece, and grows rapidly. An artificial eye has been inserted in this piece, which is comparatively rare in modern topiary although common in the Renaissance period.

These 'frames' from William Wood of Taplow, Bucks, were made of galvanised wire gauge by 1938.

Wooden frames (called formers) for creating topiary shapes were available by at least the sixteenth century, possibly earlier. A combination of evergreen plant and framework gave rise to the name 'carpenter's work' being used for some types of topiary, in particular framed doorways, arches and columns or pillars, where the woodwork might be allowed to show to give an added architectural feel. For more complex shapes such as birds or beasts, the wooden frame would be placed over the young plant (or part of the plant if only the crown was to be shaped) before it had grown, and as the plant grew into and beyond the limits of the frame it would be clipped to shape. Small flexible stems might also be tied into shape and attached to the former. The pro-forma allowed complex shapes and designs, such as sets of chess pieces, to be accomplished by even amateur gardeners, and multiple frames might be used for specimens with several levels or shapes. Once the form was established, the wooden frame would eventually rot away, leaving no sign of the initial 'guide'. Modern topiarists can purchase specialist strip-metal frames,

Above: This perfect example of spiral topiary (to the right of the image) was just one of many forms in the gardens of Ascot (Berkshire), c. 1906.

Below: The gardens at Bridge End, Saffron Walden, date to the 1840s and were laid out by the Gibson family. They were restored in 2003. Much of the box was replaced but the vastly overgrown yews were cut back and re-sprouted. This postcard shows them prior to their decline and restoration.

or more popularly wire mesh frames in a wide variety of shapes. The wire mesh frames allow for an almost naturalistic approach, with curved surfaces abounding on life-like pigs and birds 'in flight'. Wire mesh formers appear to have been available by the mid-nineteenth century.

Spirals can be produced with the aid of string wound evenly and gradually upwards around the already formed column, and fastigiate forms of fine-leaved evergreens are best for this, such as yew, although box will also give good results. A true spiral will allow the main upright stem to show and the spiral to be clipped into a rounded curve, giving the impression of a rather plump boa constrictor embracing a pole. Most complex and time-consuming are the styles of topiary that allow a view of the stem of the plant as part of the form, for example the popular 'cake-stand' or 'crown and ball'. The exposed stem has to be discouraged from producing side stems by laborious and detailed bud-rubbing on the main stem each spring.

In the Edwardian period, large topiary gardens might take several men nine to ten weeks to clip. Commencing as soon as possible after September, three or four experienced gardeners would be put to work in time to finish before the severe frosts of winter set in. Box was particularly prone to frost. Scaffolding or trestles were used for the larger trees, with a panoply of strings, battens, spirit levels, guides, etc. Exactitude within a matter of a degree was essential in hedging, with most hedges widening towards the base, allowing air and light from the slightly narrower top. Novice gardeners would be put to work alongside the more experienced men to learn their trade. Hedges, rather than shapes, were considered the most difficult to clip perfectly, with high standards exacted in the country house garden. Substantial re-shaping of older trees or renovating was not generally recommended and even now is a subject of considerable debate in historic garden restorations. Plants under any stress may not survive severe cutting. At Wrest Park (Beds), mature yew hedging that may have dated to the early eighteenth century or earlier died back after cutting back due to a combination of shock, wind exposure and water-logging in a wet year, but a similar exercise at Bridge End Gardens, Saffron Walden (Essex) proved a success.

Accessing the top of tall topiary can be a challenge! In the early twentieth century Mr Prucha had to reach over 15 feet to clip his extensive topiary menagerie in his gardens in Neb, Crete.

TOPIARY GARDENS TO VISIT

Athelhampton House, Athelhampton, Dorchester, Dorset DT2 7LG
Website: www.athelhampton.co.uk
The famous 20-foot high pyramidal yews at Athelhampton began life as much smaller decorations within the formal gardens.

Chastleton House, Chastleton, Moreton-in-Marsh, Oxfordshire GL56 0SU
Website: www.nationaltrust.org.uk/main/w-chastleton
The box figures here are placed within a retaining hedge.

Clipsham Yew Tree Avenue, Near Clipsham, Lincolnshire.
Website: www.timaps.co.uk/place?pl=clipsham-yew-tree-avenue
The half-mile-long avenue now owned by the Forestry Commission, contains almost 150 clipped yews, some of which are 200 years old.

Elvaston Castle, Near Derby, Derbyshire DE72 3EP.
Website: www.elvastoncastle.org.uk
The original inspiration for nineteenth-century topiary revival.

Erdigg, Wrexham, Clwyd, Wales LL13 0YT.
Website: www.nationaltrust.org.uk/main/w-erddig
Substantial historic yew specimens.

Great Dixter, Northiam, Rye, East Sussex TN31 6PH
Website: www.greatdixter.co.uk
Originally created by Nathaniel Lloyd, author of *Garden Craftsmanship in Yew and Box*, the topiary now forms a backdrop for the gardens of plantsman Christopher Lloyd.

Hatfield House, Hatfield, Hertfordshire AL9 5NQ
Website: www.hatfield-house.co.uk
The gardens contain a series of formal areas with clipped work and a yew maze to the east front contains topiary lions.

Hever Castle, Hever, Nr Edenbridge, Kent TN8 7NG
Website: www.hevercastle.co.uk
One of the best surviving examples of the work of the Cheal's nursery.

Levens Hall, Kendall, Cumbria LA8 0PD.
Website: www.levenshall.co.uk
The gardens, and original formal planting, were laid out between 1689 and 1720.

Nymans, Haywards Heath, West Sussex RH12 6EB
Website: www.nationaltrust.org.uk/main/w-nymansgarden2
The yew pillared orbs were created as part of the walled garden by the plant-collecting Messel family in 1904.

Owlpen, Uley, Gloucestershire GL11 5BZ
Website: www.owlpen.com
A distinctive Arts and Crafts garden with much clipped work.

Powys Castle and Garden, Welshpool, Wales SY21 8RF

> Website: www.nationaltrust.org.uk/main/w-powiscastle_garden
> World-famous terraced gardens with ancient clipped yews.

Rodmarton Manor, Cirencester, Gloucestershire GL7 6PF

> Website: www.rodmarton-manor.co.uk
> A site of interest for its Arts and Crafts and associations with John Sedding and Reginald Blomfield.

BIBLIOGRAPHY

Baker, Margaret. *Discovering Topiary*. Shire Publications, Bucks, 1969.

Benton, Alison. *Cheals of Crawley*. Moira Publications, Sussex, 2002.

Blomfield, Reginald. *The Formal Garden in England*. Republished in 1985 by Waterstone, London, 1892 (republished 1995).

Briggs, C. Stephen, and Peter Davies. 'Garden Topiary and Ornamental Shrub Cutting on Welsh Post Cards', in *Gerddii* (The Journal of the Welsh Historic Gardens Trust) Vol. V, 2008–9, pp. 73–90.

Clarke, Ethne, and George Wright. *English Topiary Gardens*. Phoenix Illustrated, London, 1997.

Curtis, Charles H., and Gibson, W. *The Book of Topiary*. John Lane: The Bodley Head, London and New York, 1904.

Johnson, George W. *History of Gardening*. Baldwin & Cradock, 1829.

Lawson, William. *A New Orchard and Garden with The Country Housewife's Garden*. (1618) (facsimile published 2003, Prospect Books).

Lloyd, Nathaniel. *Garden Craftsmanship in Yew and Box*. Country Life, London, 1925.

Mathews, W. H. *Mazes and Labyrinths*. Dover Publications, London, 1922.

Robinson, William. *The English Flower Garden*. (15th edition 1933) J. Murray, London.

Sedding, John. *Garden Craft Old and New*. K. Paul, Trench, Trübner & Co., Ltd, London, 1891.

Stewart, Cecil. *Topiary: An Historical Diversion*. The Golden Cockerel Press, London, 1956.

Topiarius (The Journal of the European Boxwood and Topiary Society)

Whalley, Robin and Jennings, Anne. *Knot Gardens and Parterres*. Barn Elms, London, 1998.

WEBSITES

www.topiary.org.uk International association of topiary growers and suppliers.

www.frostatmidnight.co.uk A site with a short history of topiary and descriptions of topiary gardens in each county of England.

INDEX

Page numbers in italic refer to illustrations